This book belongs to
Cara

Aesop's Fables

The Hare and the Tortoise & Other Fables

Retold by Andrea Stacy Leach
Illustrated by Holly Hannon

Exclusive distribution by Paradise Press, Inc.
Created and manufactured by arrangement with Ottenheimer Publishers, Inc.

The Fables

The Hare and the Tortoise

One day the hare was boasting to his friends about his speed.

"I challenge anyone here to race with me," he said.

To the hare's surprise, the tortoise said, "I accept your challenge."

"Don't be silly," said the hare. "I can run circles around you and still win."

"Save your boasting until the end of the race," warned the tortoise. "Are you ready?"

The course was set, and the race began. The hare moved quickly into the lead. He laughed over his shoulder at the tortoise's slow pace.

The hare sped away. When he could no longer see the tortoise, he began to run lazily. "I might as well take a nap," he said to himself. "If the tortoise overtakes me, I can always catch up and win the race."

Meanwhile, the tortoise plodded on at a slow and steady pace. He quietly passed the hare but did not stop to rest.

When the foolish hare woke up from his nap, he didn't see the tortoise anywhere. So he raced to the finish line, but found that he was too late. The tortoise had already won the race!

Slow and steady wins the race.

The Town Mouse and the Country Mouse

One day the town mouse decided to visit his cousin in the country.

"Welcome!" exclaimed the country mouse when he saw his cousin. He invited him to sit and eat. Beans with bacon and some cheese and bread were all he had, but he shared them freely.

Before long the town mouse said, "Cousin, why do you live out here in the country eating this simple food? Come with me to town, and I will show you how to live!"

The country mouse soon agreed, and they set off.

When they arrived, the town mouse said, "Cousin, I'm sure you are hungry after our long trip," and showed him the dining room. A lovely feast had just ended, and there were delicious cakes and jellies to eat.

Suddenly the door opened, and in came two large dogs, barking loudly. The two mice ran away and hid.

"Goodbye, cousin," said the country mouse.

"What? Going so soon?" the town mouse asked.

But the country mouse did not answer. He was already gone, on his way back to his quiet life.

Better to eat beans and bacon in peace
than cakes and jellies in fear.

The Farmer's Daughter

The farmer's daughter was on her way to market, carrying a pail of milk on her head. She began to think about how she would spend the money from the sale of the milk.

"I will buy some lovely hens, and they will lay many eggs," she thought. "Chicks will hatch from the eggs, and I will feed and care for them."

Just then, she came upon a ditch in the road. She took care in stepping around the ditch so she would not spill the milk.

"And when the chicks are grown," she continued, "I will sell them at the market. With the money I make, I will buy a new frock and some pretty ribbons to wear to the fair. All the young men will want to dance with me. But I will pretend not to notice them. I'll toss my head, as if I don't care."

But as she tossed her head, down came the milk pail! The farmer's daughter began to cry over the spilt milk. All she had left were her empty pail and the promise of a scolding when she reached home.

Don't count your chickens before they are hatched.

The Fox and the Crow

A fox spied a crow flying with a piece of cheese in its beak. The crow settled on a nearby branch and prepared to eat its meal.

"Ah, that's for me," said the fox to himself. He walked under the tree.

"Good morning Mistress Crow!" he said. "My, how lovely you are looking today! Your eyes are so bright and your feathers so glossy. I feel certain your voice is more beautiful than any other bird's. How I long to hear it for myself, O Queen of Birds."

The crow became so proud and pleased by his words that she opened her mouth to sing.

"Caw, caw!" she began, and the cheese fell from her beak. The fox snatched it up and said, "Thank you. This was all I really wanted." And he trotted away.

Never trust a flatterer.